SKYDIVING
LOG BOOK

Name: _____

Phone #: _____

Adress: _____

Email: _____

Height: _____ Weight: _____

*"Life begins at the end of
your comfort zone."*

SKYDIVE INDEX

N°	Location - Date

N°	Location - Date

N°	Location - Date

SKYDIVE LOG

N°

Date: _____ Time: _____

Location: _____

Weather: ☀ ☁ ⛅ 🌧 Temperature: _____

The Jump

Type of jump: _____ Aircraft: _____

Equipment: _____

Alt. Exit: _____

Alt. Deployment: _____

Freefall Duration: _____

Total Freefall Time: _____

Signature

Comments & Rating

_____
_____
_____

Overall Rating
★ ★ ★ ★ ★

SKYDIVE LOG

N°

Date: _____ Time: _____

Location: _____

Weather: ☀ ☁ ⛅ 🌧 Temperature: _____

The Jump

Type of jump: _____ Aircraft: _____

Equipment: _____

Alt. Exit: _____

Alt. Deployment: _____

Freefall Duration: _____

Total Freefall Time: _____

Signature

Comments & Rating

_____
_____
_____

Overall Rating
★ ★ ★ ★ ★

SKYDIVE LOG

N°

Date: _____ Time: _____

Location: _____

Weather: ☀ ☁ ⛅ 🌧 Temperature: _____

The Jump

Type of jump: _____ Aircraft: _____

Equipment: _____

Alt. Exit: _____

Alt. Deployment: _____

Freefall Duration: _____

Total Freefall Time: _____

Signature

Comments & Rating

_____

_____

_____

Overall Rating

⭐ ⭐ ⭐ ⭐ ⭐

SKYDIVE LOG

N°

Date: _____ Time: _____

Location: _____

Weather: ☀ ☁ ⛅ 🌧 Temperature: _____

The Jump

Type of jump: _____ Aircraft: _____

Equipment: _____

Alt. Exit: _____

Alt. Deployment: _____

Freefall Duration: _____

Total Freefall Time: _____

Signature

Comments & Rating

_____

_____

_____

Overall Rating

⭐ ⭐ ⭐ ⭐ ⭐

SKYDIVE LOG

N°

Date: _____ Time: _____

Location: _____

Weather: ☀ ☁ ⛅ 🌧 Temperature: _____

The Jump

Type of jump: _____ Aircraft: _____

Equipment: _____

Alt. Exit: _____

Alt. Deployment: _____

Freefall Duration: _____

Total Freefall Time: _____

Signature

Comments & Rating

_____

_____

_____

Overall Rating

⭐ ⭐ ⭐ ⭐ ⭐

SKYDIVE LOG

N°

Date: _____ Time: _____

Location: _____

Weather: ☀ ☁ ⛅ 🌧 Temperature: _____

The Jump

Type of jump: _____ Aircraft: _____

Equipment: _____

Alt. Exit: _____

Alt. Deployment: _____

Freefall Duration: _____

Total Freefall Time: _____

Signature

Comments & Rating

_____

_____

_____

Overall Rating

⭐ ⭐ ⭐ ⭐ ⭐

SKYDIVE LOG N°

Date: _____ Time: _____

Location: _____

Weather: ☀ ☁ ⛅ 🌧 Temperature: _____

The Jump

Type of jump: _____ Aircraft: _____

Equipment: _____

Alt. Exit: _____ Signature

Alt. Deployment: _____

Freefall Duration: _____

Total Freefall Time: _____

Comments & Rating

_____ Overall Rating

_____ ⭐ ⭐ ⭐ ⭐ ⭐

_____

SKYDIVE LOG N°

Date: _____ Time: _____

Location: _____

Weather: ☀ ☁ ⛅ 🌧 Temperature: _____

The Jump

Type of jump: _____ Aircraft: _____

Equipment: _____

Alt. Exit: _____ Signature

Alt. Deployment: _____

Freefall Duration: _____

Total Freefall Time: _____

Comments & Rating

_____ Overall Rating

_____ ⭐ ⭐ ⭐ ⭐ ⭐

_____

SKYDIVE LOG N°

Date: _____ Time: _____

Location: _____

Weather: ☀ ☁ ⛅ 🌧 Temperature: _____

The Jump

Type of jump: _____ Aircraft: _____

Equipment: _____

Alt. Exit: _____

Alt. Deployment: _____

Freefall Duration: _____

Total Freefall Time: _____

Signature

Comments & Rating

_____

_____

_____

Overall Rating

⭐ ⭐ ⭐ ⭐ ⭐

SKYDIVE LOG N°

Date: _____ Time: _____

Location: _____

Weather: ☀ ☁ ⛅ 🌧 Temperature: _____

The Jump

Type of jump: _____ Aircraft: _____

Equipment: _____

Alt. Exit: _____

Alt. Deployment: _____

Freefall Duration: _____

Total Freefall Time: _____

Signature

Comments & Rating

_____

_____

_____

Overall Rating

⭐ ⭐ ⭐ ⭐ ⭐

SKYDIVE LOG

N°

Date: _____ Time: _____

Location: _____

Weather: ☀ ☁ ⛅ 🌧 Temperature: _____

The Jump

Type of jump: _____ Aircraft: _____

Equipment: _____

Alt. Exit: _____ Signature

Alt. Deployment: _____

Freefall Duration: _____

Total Freefall Time: _____

Comments & Rating

_____

_____ Overall Rating

_____ ⭐ ⭐ ⭐ ⭐ ⭐

SKYDIVE LOG

N°

Date: _____ Time: _____

Location: _____

Weather: ☀ ☁ ⛅ 🌧 Temperature: _____

The Jump

Type of jump: _____ Aircraft: _____

Equipment: _____

Alt. Exit: _____ Signature

Alt. Deployment: _____

Freefall Duration: _____

Total Freefall Time: _____

Comments & Rating

_____

_____ Overall Rating

_____ ⭐ ⭐ ⭐ ⭐ ⭐

SKYDIVE LOG

N°

Date: _____ Time: _____

Location: _____

Weather: ☀ ☁ ⛅ 🌧 Temperature: _____

The Jump

Type of jump: _____ Aircraft: _____

Equipment: _____

Alt. Exit: _____

Signature

Alt. Deployment: _____

Freefall Duration: _____

Total Freefall Time: _____

Comments & Rating

_____

_____ Overall Rating

_____ ☆ ☆ ☆ ☆ ☆

SKYDIVE LOG

N°

Date: _____ Time: _____

Location: _____

Weather: ☀ ☁ ⛅ 🌧 Temperature: _____

The Jump

Type of jump: _____ Aircraft: _____

Equipment: _____

Alt. Exit: _____

Signature

Alt. Deployment: _____

Freefall Duration: _____

Total Freefall Time: _____

Comments & Rating

_____

_____ Overall Rating

_____ ☆ ☆ ☆ ☆ ☆

SKYDIVE LOG   N°

Date: _____ Time: _____

Location: _____

Weather: ☀ ☁ ⛅ 🌧 Temperature: _____

The Jump

Type of jump: _____ Aircraft: _____

Equipment: _____

Alt. Exit: _____   Signature

Alt. Deployment: _____

Freefall Duration: _____

Total Freefall Time: _____

Comments & Rating

_____   Overall Rating
_____   ☆ ☆ ☆ ☆ ☆
_____

SKYDIVE LOG   N°

Date: _____ Time: _____

Location: _____

Weather: ☀ ☁ ⛅ 🌧 Temperature: _____

The Jump

Type of jump: _____ Aircraft: _____

Equipment: _____

Alt. Exit: _____   Signature

Alt. Deployment: _____

Freefall Duration: _____

Total Freefall Time: _____

Comments & Rating

_____   Overall Rating
_____   ☆ ☆ ☆ ☆ ☆

SKYDIVE LOG

N°

Date: _____ Time: _____

Location: _____

Weather: ☀ ☁ ⛅ 🌧 Temperature: _____

The Jump

Type of jump: _____ Aircraft: _____

Equipment: _____

Alt. Exit: _____

Alt. Deployment: _____

Freefall Duration: _____

Total Freefall Time: _____

Signature

Comments & Rating

_____

_____

_____

Overall Rating

⭐ ⭐ ⭐ ⭐ ⭐

SKYDIVE LOG

N°

Date: _____ Time: _____

Location: _____

Weather: ☀ ☁ ⛅ 🌧 Temperature: _____

The Jump

Type of jump: _____ Aircraft: _____

Equipment: _____

Alt. Exit: _____

Alt. Deployment: _____

Freefall Duration: _____

Total Freefall Time: _____

Signature

Comments & Rating

_____

_____

_____

Overall Rating

⭐ ⭐ ⭐ ⭐ ⭐

SKYDIVE LOG

N°

Date: _____ Time: _____
Location: _____
Weather: ☀ ☁ ⛅ 🌧 Temperature: _____

The Jump

Type of jump: _____ Aircraft: _____
Equipment: _____
Alt. Exit: _____
Alt. Deployment: _____
Freefall Duration: _____
Total Freefall Time: _____

Signature

Comments & Rating

_____
_____
_____

Overall Rating
⭐ ⭐ ⭐ ⭐ ⭐

SKYDIVE LOG

N°

Date: _____ Time: _____
Location: _____
Weather: ☀ ☁ ⛅ 🌧 Temperature: _____

The Jump

Type of jump: _____ Aircraft: _____
Equipment: _____
Alt. Exit: _____
Alt. Deployment: _____
Freefall Duration: _____
Total Freefall Time: _____

Signature

Comments & Rating

_____
_____
_____

Overall Rating
⭐ ⭐ ⭐ ⭐ ⭐

SKYDIVE LOG

N°

Date: _____ Time: _____

Location: _____

Weather: ☀ ☁ ⛅ 🌧 Temperature: _____

The Jump

Type of jump: _____ Aircraft: _____

Equipment: _____

Alt. Exit: _____

Alt. Deployment: _____

Freefall Duration: _____

Total Freefall Time: _____

Signature

Comments & Rating

_____

_____

_____

Overall Rating

⭐ ⭐ ⭐ ⭐ ⭐

SKYDIVE LOG

N°

Date: _____ Time: _____

Location: _____

Weather: ☀ ☁ ⛅ 🌧 Temperature: _____

The Jump

Type of jump: _____ Aircraft: _____

Equipment: _____

Alt. Exit: _____

Alt. Deployment: _____

Freefall Duration: _____

Total Freefall Time: _____

Signature

Comments & Rating

_____

_____

_____

Overall Rating

⭐ ⭐ ⭐ ⭐ ⭐

SKYDIVE LOG

Date: _____ Time: _____

Location: _____

Weather: ☀ ☁ ⛅ 🌧 Temperature: _____

The Jump

Type of jump: _____ Aircraft: _____

Equipment: _____

Alt. Exit: _____

Signature

Alt. Deployment: _____

Freefall Duration: _____

Total Freefall Time: _____

Comments & Rating

_____

_____

Overall Rating

_____ ⭐ ⭐ ⭐ ⭐ ⭐

SKYDIVE LOG

Date: _____ Time: _____

Location: _____

Weather: ☀ ☁ ⛅ 🌧 Temperature: _____

The Jump

Type of jump: _____ Aircraft: _____

Equipment: _____

Alt. Exit: _____

Signature

Alt. Deployment: _____

Freefall Duration: _____

Total Freefall Time: _____

Comments & Rating

_____

_____

Overall Rating

_____ ⭐ ⭐ ⭐ ⭐ ⭐

SKYDIVE LOG   N°

Date: _____ Time: _____

Location: _____

Weather: ☀ ☁ ⛅ 🌧 Temperature: _____

The Jump

Type of jump: _____ Aircraft: _____

Equipment: _____

Alt. Exit: _____

Alt. Deployment: _____   Signature

Freefall Duration: _____   ┌─────────────────┐
                                │   │
Total Freefall Time: _____   └─────────────────┘

Comments & Rating

_____

_____   Overall Rating

_____   ⭐ ⭐ ⭐ ⭐ ⭐

SKYDIVE LOG   N°

Date: _____ Time: _____

Location: _____

Weather: ☀ ☁ ⛅ 🌧 Temperature: _____

The Jump

Type of jump: _____ Aircraft: _____

Equipment: _____

Alt. Exit: _____

Alt. Deployment: _____   Signature

Freefall Duration: _____   ┌─────────────────┐
                                │   │
Total Freefall Time: _____   └─────────────────┘

Comments & Rating

_____

_____   Overall Rating

_____   ⭐ ⭐ ⭐ ⭐ ⭐

SKYDIVE LOG

N°

Date: .... Time: ....

Location: ....

Weather: ☀ ☁ ⛅ 🌧 Temperature: ....

The Jump

Type of jump: .... Aircraft: ....

Equipment: ....

Alt. Exit: ....

Signature

Alt. Deployment: ....

Freefall Duration: ....

Total Freefall Time: ....

Comments & Rating

....

Overall Rating

.... ☆ ☆ ☆ ☆ ☆

....

SKYDIVE LOG

N°

Date: .... Time: ....

Location: ....

Weather: ☀ ☁ ⛅ 🌧 Temperature: ....

The Jump

Type of jump: .... Aircraft: ....

Equipment: ....

Alt. Exit: ....

Signature

Alt. Deployment: ....

Freefall Duration: ....

Total Freefall Time: ....

Comments & Rating

....

Overall Rating

.... ☆ ☆ ☆ ☆ ☆

....

SKYDIVE LOG   N°

Date: _____ Time: _____

Location: _____

Weather: ☀ ☁ ⛅ 🌧 Temperature: _____

The Jump

Type of jump: _____ Aircraft: _____

Equipment: _____

Alt. Exit: _____

Alt. Deployment: _____   Signature

Freefall Duration: _____

Total Freefall Time: _____

Comments & Rating

_____

_____   Overall Rating

_____   ⭐ ⭐ ⭐ ⭐ ⭐

SKYDIVE LOG   N°

Date: _____ Time: _____

Location: _____

Weather: ☀ ☁ ⛅ 🌧 Temperature: _____

The Jump

Type of jump: _____ Aircraft: _____

Equipment: _____

Alt. Exit: _____

Alt. Deployment: _____   Signature

Freefall Duration: _____

Total Freefall Time: _____

Comments & Rating

_____

_____   Overall Rating

_____   ⭐ ⭐ ⭐ ⭐ ⭐

SKYDIVE LOG N°

Date: _____ Time: _____

Location: _____

Weather: ☀ ☁ 🌤 🌧 Temperature: _____

The Jump

Type of jump: _____ Aircraft: _____

Equipment: _____

Alt. Exit: _____ Signature

Alt. Deployment: _____

Freefall Duration: _____

Total Freefall Time: _____

Comments & Rating

_____

_____ Overall Rating

_____ ⭐ ⭐ ⭐ ⭐ ⭐

SKYDIVE LOG N°

Date: _____ Time: _____

Location: _____

Weather: ☀ ☁ 🌤 🌧 Temperature: _____

The Jump

Type of jump: _____ Aircraft: _____

Equipment: _____

Alt. Exit: _____ Signature

Alt. Deployment: _____

Freefall Duration: _____

Total Freefall Time: _____

Comments & Rating

_____

_____ Overall Rating

_____ ⭐ ⭐ ⭐ ⭐ ⭐

SKYDIVE LOG N°

Date: _____ Time: _____

Location: _____

Weather: ☀ ☁ ⛅ 🌧 Temperature: _____

The Jump

Type of jump: _____ Aircraft: _____

Equipment: _____

Alt. Exit: _____

Alt. Deployment: _____

Freefall Duration: _____

Total Freefall Time: _____

Signature

Comments & Rating

_____

_____

_____

Overall Rating

⭐ ⭐ ⭐ ⭐ ⭐

SKYDIVE LOG N°

Date: _____ Time: _____

Location: _____

Weather: ☀ ☁ ⛅ 🌧 Temperature: _____

The Jump

Type of jump: _____ Aircraft: _____

Equipment: _____

Alt. Exit: _____

Alt. Deployment: _____

Freefall Duration: _____

Total Freefall Time: _____

Signature

Comments & Rating

_____

_____

_____

Overall Rating

⭐ ⭐ ⭐ ⭐ ⭐

SKYDIVE LOG

N°

Date: _____ Time: _____

Location: _____

Weather: ☀ ☁ ⛅ 🌧 Temperature: _____

The Jump

Type of jump: _____ Aircraft: _____

Equipment: _____

Alt. Exit: _____

Alt. Deployment: _____

Freefall Duration: _____

Total Freefall Time: _____

Signature

Comments & Rating

_____

_____

_____

Overall Rating

⭐ ⭐ ⭐ ⭐ ⭐

SKYDIVE LOG

N°

Date: _____ Time: _____

Location: _____

Weather: ☀ ☁ ⛅ 🌧 Temperature: _____

The Jump

Type of jump: _____ Aircraft: _____

Equipment: _____

Alt. Exit: _____

Alt. Deployment: _____

Freefall Duration: _____

Total Freefall Time: _____

Signature

Comments & Rating

_____

_____

_____

Overall Rating

⭐ ⭐ ⭐ ⭐ ⭐

SKYDIVE LOG
N°

Date: _____ Time: _____
Location: _____
Weather: ☀ ☁ ⛅ 🌧 Temperature: _____

The Jump

Type of jump: _____ Aircraft: _____
Equipment: _____
Alt. Exit: _____
Alt. Deployment: _____
Freefall Duration: _____
Total Freefall Time: _____

Signature

Comments & Rating

_____
_____
_____

Overall Rating
⭐ ⭐ ⭐ ⭐ ⭐

SKYDIVE LOG
N°

Date: _____ Time: _____
Location: _____
Weather: ☀ ☁ ⛅ 🌧 Temperature: _____

The Jump

Type of jump: _____ Aircraft: _____
Equipment: _____
Alt. Exit: _____
Alt. Deployment: _____
Freefall Duration: _____
Total Freefall Time: _____

Signature

Comments & Rating

_____
_____
_____

Overall Rating
⭐ ⭐ ⭐ ⭐ ⭐

SKYDIVE LOG

N°

Date: _____ Time: _____

Location: _____

Weather: ☀ ☁ 🌤 🌧 Temperature: _____

The Jump

Type of jump: _____ Aircraft: _____

Equipment: _____

Alt. Exit: _____

Alt. Deployment: _____

Freefall Duration: _____

Total Freefall Time: _____

Signature

Comments & Rating

_____

_____

_____

Overall Rating

⭐ ⭐ ⭐ ⭐ ⭐

SKYDIVE LOG

N°

Date: _____ Time: _____

Location: _____

Weather: ☀ ☁ 🌤 🌧 Temperature: _____

The Jump

Type of jump: _____ Aircraft: _____

Equipment: _____

Alt. Exit: _____

Alt. Deployment: _____

Freefall Duration: _____

Total Freefall Time: _____

Signature

Comments & Rating

_____

_____

_____

Overall Rating

⭐ ⭐ ⭐ ⭐ ⭐

SKYDIVE LOG

N°

Date: _____ Time: _____

Location: _____

Weather: ☀ ☁ ⛅ 🌧 Temperature: _____

The Jump

Type of jump: _____ Aircraft: _____

Equipment: _____

Alt. Exit: _____

Alt. Deployment: _____

Freefall Duration: _____

Total Freefall Time: _____

Signature

Comments & Rating

_____

_____

_____

Overall Rating

⭐ ⭐ ⭐ ⭐ ⭐

SKYDIVE LOG

N°

Date: _____ Time: _____

Location: _____

Weather: ☀ ☁ ⛅ 🌧 Temperature: _____

The Jump

Type of jump: _____ Aircraft: _____

Equipment: _____

Alt. Exit: _____

Alt. Deployment: _____

Freefall Duration: _____

Total Freefall Time: _____

Signature

Comments & Rating

_____

_____

_____

Overall Rating

⭐ ⭐ ⭐ ⭐ ⭐

SKYDIVE LOG

N°

Date: _____ Time: _____

Location: _____

Weather: ☀ ☁ ⛅ 🌧 Temperature: _____

The Jump

Type of jump: _____ Aircraft: _____

Equipment: _____

Alt. Exit: _____

Alt. Deployment: _____

Freefall Duration: _____

Total Freefall Time: _____

Signature

Comments & Rating

_____

_____

_____

Overall Rating

⭐ ⭐ ⭐ ⭐ ⭐

SKYDIVE LOG

N°

Date: _____ Time: _____

Location: _____

Weather: ☀ ☁ ⛅ 🌧 Temperature: _____

The Jump

Type of jump: _____ Aircraft: _____

Equipment: _____

Alt. Exit: _____

Alt. Deployment: _____

Freefall Duration: _____

Total Freefall Time: _____

Signature

Comments & Rating

_____

_____

_____

Overall Rating

⭐ ⭐ ⭐ ⭐ ⭐

SKYDIVE LOG
N°

Date: _____ Time: _____
Location: _____
Weather: ☀ ☁ ⛅ 🌧 Temperature: _____

The Jump

Type of jump: _____ Aircraft: _____
Equipment: _____
Alt. Exit: _____
Alt. Deployment: _____
Freefall Duration: _____
Total Freefall Time: _____

Signature

Comments & Rating

_____
_____
_____

Overall Rating
⭐ ⭐ ⭐ ⭐ ⭐

SKYDIVE LOG
N°

Date: _____ Time: _____
Location: _____
Weather: ☀ ☁ ⛅ 🌧 Temperature: _____

The Jump

Type of jump: _____ Aircraft: _____
Equipment: _____
Alt. Exit: _____
Alt. Deployment: _____
Freefall Duration: _____
Total Freefall Time: _____

Signature

Comments & Rating

_____
_____
_____

Overall Rating
⭐ ⭐ ⭐ ⭐ ⭐

SKYDIVE LOG

N°

Date: _____ Time: _____

Location: _____

Weather: ☀ ☁ ⛅ 🌧 Temperature: _____

The Jump

Type of jump: _____ Aircraft: _____

Equipment: _____

Alt. Exit: _____

Signature

Alt. Deployment: _____

Freefall Duration: _____

Total Freefall Time: _____

Comments & Rating

_____

_____

_____

Overall Rating

⭐ ⭐ ⭐ ⭐ ⭐

SKYDIVE LOG

N°

Date: _____ Time: _____

Location: _____

Weather: ☀ ☁ ⛅ 🌧 Temperature: _____

The Jump

Type of jump: _____ Aircraft: _____

Equipment: _____

Alt. Exit: _____

Signature

Alt. Deployment: _____

Freefall Duration: _____

Total Freefall Time: _____

Comments & Rating

_____

_____

Overall Rating

⭐ ⭐ ⭐ ⭐ ⭐

SKYDIVE LOG   N° ☐

Date: _____ Time: _____

Location: _____

Weather: ☀ ☁ ⛅ 🌧 Temperature: _____

The Jump

Type of jump: _____ Aircraft: _____

Equipment: _____

Alt. Exit: _____

Alt. Deployment: _____

Freefall Duration: _____

Total Freefall Time: _____

Signature
☐

Comments & Rating

_____

_____

_____

Overall Rating
⭐ ⭐ ⭐ ⭐ ⭐

SKYDIVE LOG   N° ☐

Date: _____ Time: _____

Location: _____

Weather: ☀ ☁ ⛅ 🌧 Temperature: _____

The Jump

Type of jump: _____ Aircraft: _____

Equipment: _____

Alt. Exit: _____

Alt. Deployment: _____

Freefall Duration: _____

Total Freefall Time: _____

Signature
☐

Comments & Rating

_____

_____

_____

Overall Rating
⭐ ⭐ ⭐ ⭐ ⭐

SKYDIVE LOG   N° ☐

Date: _____ Time: _____

Location: _____

Weather: ☀ ☁ ⛅ ⛈ Temperature: _____

The Jump

Type of jump: _____ Aircraft: _____

Equipment: _____

Alt. Exit: _____

Alt. Deployment: _____   Signature

Freefall Duration: _____

Total Freefall Time: _____

Comments & Rating

_____   Overall Rating

_____   ★ ★ ★ ★ ★

_____

SKYDIVE LOG   N° ☐

Date: _____ Time: _____

Location: _____

Weather: ☀ ☁ ⛅ ⛈ Temperature: _____

The Jump

Type of jump: _____ Aircraft: _____

Equipment: _____

Alt. Exit: _____

Alt. Deployment: _____   Signature

Freefall Duration: _____

Total Freefall Time: _____

Comments & Rating

_____   Overall Rating

_____   ★ ★ ★ ★ ★

_____

SKYDIVE LOG N°

Date: _____ Time: _____
Location: _____
Weather: ☀ ☁ 🌤 🌧 Temperature: _____

The Jump

Type of jump: _____ Aircraft: _____
Equipment: _____
Alt. Exit: _____
Alt. Deployment: _____
Freefall Duration: _____
Total Freefall Time: _____

Signature

Comments & Rating

_____
_____
_____

Overall Rating
⭐ ⭐ ⭐ ⭐ ⭐

SKYDIVE LOG N°

Date: _____ Time: _____
Location: _____
Weather: ☀ ☁ 🌤 🌧 Temperature: _____

The Jump

Type of jump: _____ Aircraft: _____
Equipment: _____
Alt. Exit: _____
Alt. Deployment: _____
Freefall Duration: _____
Total Freefall Time: _____

Signature

Comments & Rating

_____
_____
_____

Overall Rating
⭐ ⭐ ⭐ ⭐ ⭐

SKYDIVE LOG N° ☐

Date: _____ Time: _____

Location: _____

Weather: ☀ ☁ ⛅ 🌧 Temperature: _____

The Jump

Type of jump: _____ Aircraft: _____

Equipment: _____

Alt. Exit: _____   Signature

Alt. Deployment: _____

Freefall Duration: _____

Total Freefall Time: _____

Comments & Rating

_____

_____   Overall Rating

_____   ★ ★ ★ ★ ★

SKYDIVE LOG N° ☐

Date: _____ Time: _____

Location: _____

Weather: ☀ ☁ ⛅ 🌧 Temperature: _____

The Jump

Type of jump: _____ Aircraft: _____

Equipment: _____

Alt. Exit: _____   Signature

Alt. Deployment: _____

Freefall Duration: _____

Total Freefall Time: _____

Comments & Rating

_____

_____   Overall Rating

_____   ★ ★ ★ ★ ★

SKYDIVE LOG

N°

Date: _____ Time: _____

Location: _____

Weather: ☀ ☁ ⛅ 🌧 Temperature: _____

The Jump

Type of jump: _____ Aircraft: _____

Equipment: _____

Alt. Exit: _____

Signature

Alt. Deployment: _____

Freefall Duration: _____

Total Freefall Time: _____

Comments & Rating

_____

_____   Overall Rating

_____   ⭐ ⭐ ⭐ ⭐ ⭐

SKYDIVE LOG

N°

Date: _____ Time: _____

Location: _____

Weather: ☀ ☁ ⛅ 🌧 Temperature: _____

The Jump

Type of jump: _____ Aircraft: _____

Equipment: _____

Alt. Exit: _____

Signature

Alt. Deployment: _____

Freefall Duration: _____

Total Freefall Time: _____

Comments & Rating

_____

_____   Overall Rating

_____   ⭐ ⭐ ⭐ ⭐ ⭐

SKYDIVE LOG

N°

Date: _____ Time: _____

Location: _____

Weather: ☀ ☁ ⛅ 🌧 Temperature: _____

The Jump

Type of jump: _____ Aircraft: _____

Equipment: _____

Alt. Exit: _____

Alt. Deployment: _____

Freefall Duration: _____

Total Freefall Time: _____

Signature

Comments & Rating

_____

_____

_____

Overall Rating

⭐ ⭐ ⭐ ⭐ ⭐

SKYDIVE LOG

N°

Date: _____ Time: _____

Location: _____

Weather: ☀ ☁ ⛅ 🌧 Temperature: _____

The Jump

Type of jump: _____ Aircraft: _____

Equipment: _____

Alt. Exit: _____

Alt. Deployment: _____

Freefall Duration: _____

Total Freefall Time: _____

Signature

Comments & Rating

_____

_____

_____

Overall Rating

⭐ ⭐ ⭐ ⭐ ⭐

SKYDIVE LOG N° ▢

Date: _____ Time: _____

Location: _____

Weather: ☀ ☁ ⛅ 🌧 Temperature: _____

The Jump

Type of jump: _____ Aircraft: _____

Equipment: _____

Alt. Exit: _____

Alt. Deployment: _____

Freefall Duration: _____

Total Freefall Time: _____

Signature

▢

Comments & Rating

_____

_____

_____

Overall Rating

⭐ ⭐ ⭐ ⭐ ⭐

SKYDIVE LOG N° ▢

Date: _____ Time: _____

Location: _____

Weather: ☀ ☁ ⛅ 🌧 Temperature: _____

The Jump

Type of jump: _____ Aircraft: _____

Equipment: _____

Alt. Exit: _____

Alt. Deployment: _____

Freefall Duration: _____

Total Freefall Time: _____

Signature

▢

Comments & Rating

_____

_____

_____

Overall Rating

⭐ ⭐ ⭐ ⭐ ⭐

SKYDIVE LOG
N°

Date: _____ Time: _____

Location: _____

Weather: ☀ ☁ ⛅ 🌧 Temperature: _____

The Jump

Type of jump: _____ Aircraft: _____

Equipment: _____

Alt. Exit: _____

Signature

Alt. Deployment: _____

Freefall Duration: _____

Total Freefall Time: _____

Comments & Rating

_____

_____

_____

Overall Rating
★ ★ ★ ★ ★

SKYDIVE LOG
N°

Date: _____ Time: _____

Location: _____

Weather: ☀ ☁ ⛅ 🌧 Temperature: _____

The Jump

Type of jump: _____ Aircraft: _____

Equipment: _____

Alt. Exit: _____

Signature

Alt. Deployment: _____

Freefall Duration: _____

Total Freefall Time: _____

Comments & Rating

_____

_____

_____

Overall Rating
★ ★ ★ ★ ★

SKYDIVE LOG

N° ☐

Date: _____ Time: _____

Location: _____

Weather: ☀ ☁ ⛅ 🌧 Temperature: _____

The Jump

Type of jump: _____ Aircraft: _____

Equipment: _____

Alt. Exit: _____

Signature

Alt. Deployment: _____

Freefall Duration: _____

Total Freefall Time: _____

Comments & Rating

_____

Overall Rating

_____

_____

⭐ ⭐ ⭐ ⭐ ⭐

SKYDIVE LOG

N° ☐

Date: _____ Time: _____

Location: _____

Weather: ☀ ☁ ⛅ 🌧 Temperature: _____

The Jump

Type of jump: _____ Aircraft: _____

Equipment: _____

Alt. Exit: _____

Signature

Alt. Deployment: _____

Freefall Duration: _____

Total Freefall Time: _____

Comments & Rating

_____

Overall Rating

_____

_____

⭐ ⭐ ⭐ ⭐ ⭐

SKYDIVE LOG
N° ☐

Date: _____ Time: _____

Location: _____

Weather: ☀ ☁ ⛅ 🌧 Temperature: _____

The Jump

Type of jump: _____ Aircraft: _____

Equipment: _____

Alt. Exit: _____

Alt. Deployment: _____

Freefall Duration: _____

Total Freefall Time: _____

Signature

Comments & Rating

_____

_____

_____

Overall Rating

⭐ ⭐ ⭐ ⭐ ⭐

SKYDIVE LOG
N° ☐

Date: _____ Time: _____

Location: _____

Weather: ☀ ☁ ⛅ 🌧 Temperature: _____

The Jump

Type of jump: _____ Aircraft: _____

Equipment: _____

Alt. Exit: _____

Alt. Deployment: _____

Freefall Duration: _____

Total Freefall Time: _____

Signature

Comments & Rating

_____

_____

_____

Overall Rating

⭐ ⭐ ⭐ ⭐ ⭐

SKYDIVE LOG N° ☐

Date: _____ Time: _____
Location: _____
Weather: ☀ ☁ ⛅ 🌧 Temperature: _____

The Jump

Type of jump: _____ Aircraft: _____
Equipment: _____
Alt. Exit: _____
Alt. Deployment: _____ Signature
Freefall Duration: _____
Total Freefall Time: _____

Comments & Rating

_____
_____ Overall Rating
_____ ★ ★ ★ ★ ★

SKYDIVE LOG N° ☐

Date: _____ Time: _____
Location: _____
Weather: ☀ ☁ ⛅ 🌧 Temperature: _____

The Jump

Type of jump: _____ Aircraft: _____
Equipment: _____
Alt. Exit: _____
Alt. Deployment: _____ Signature
Freefall Duration: _____
Total Freefall Time: _____

Comments & Rating

_____
_____ Overall Rating
_____ ★ ★ ★ ★ ★

SKYDIVE LOG   N° ☐

Date: _____   Time: _____

Location: _____

Weather: ☀ ☁ 🌤 🌧 Temperature: _____

The Jump

Type of jump: _____ Aircraft: _____

Equipment: _____

Alt. Exit: _____   Signature

Alt. Deployment: _____

Freefall Duration: _____

Total Freefall Time: _____

Comments & Rating

_____   Overall Rating

_____   ⭐ ⭐ ⭐ ⭐ ⭐

_____

SKYDIVE LOG   N° ☐

Date: _____   Time: _____

Location: _____

Weather: ☀ ☁ 🌤 🌧 Temperature: _____

The Jump

Type of jump: _____ Aircraft: _____

Equipment: _____

Alt. Exit: _____   Signature

Alt. Deployment: _____

Freefall Duration: _____

Total Freefall Time: _____

Comments & Rating

_____   Overall Rating

_____   ⭐ ⭐ ⭐ ⭐ ⭐

_____

SKYDIVE LOG

N°

Date: _____ Time: _____
Location: _____
Weather: ☀ ☁ 🌤 🌧 Temperature: _____

The Jump

Type of jump: _____ Aircraft: _____
Equipment: _____
Alt. Exit: _____

Signature

Alt. Deployment: _____
Freefall Duration: _____
Total Freefall Time: _____

Comments & Rating

_____
_____
_____

Overall Rating
★ ★ ★ ★ ★

SKYDIVE LOG

N°

Date: _____ Time: _____
Location: _____
Weather: ☀ ☁ 🌤 🌧 Temperature: _____

The Jump

Type of jump: _____ Aircraft: _____
Equipment: _____
Alt. Exit: _____

Signature

Alt. Deployment: _____
Freefall Duration: _____
Total Freefall Time: _____

Comments & Rating

_____
_____
_____

Overall Rating
★ ★ ★ ★ ★

SKYDIVE LOG   N°

Date: _____ Time: _____

Location: _____

Weather: ☀ ☁ ⛅ 🌧 Temperature: _____

The Jump

Type of jump: _____ Aircraft: _____

Equipment: _____

Alt. Exit: _____   Signature

Alt. Deployment: _____

Freefall Duration: _____

Total Freefall Time: _____

Comments & Rating

_____

_____   Overall Rating

_____   ★ ★ ★ ★ ★

SKYDIVE LOG   N°

Date: _____ Time: _____

Location: _____

Weather: ☀ ☁ ⛅ 🌧 Temperature: _____

The Jump

Type of jump: _____ Aircraft: _____

Equipment: _____

Alt. Exit: _____   Signature

Alt. Deployment: _____

Freefall Duration: _____

Total Freefall Time: _____

Comments & Rating

_____

_____   Overall Rating

_____   ★ ★ ★ ★ ★

SKYDIVE LOG

N° ☐

Date: _____ Time: _____

Location: _____

Weather: ☀ ☁ 🌤 🌧 Temperature: _____

The Jump

Type of jump: _____ Aircraft: _____

Equipment: _____

Alt. Exit: _____

Alt. Deployment: _____

Freefall Duration: _____

Total Freefall Time: _____

Signature

☐

Comments & Rating

_____

_____

Overall Rating

⭐ ⭐ ⭐ ⭐ ⭐

SKYDIVE LOG

N° ☐

Date: _____ Time: _____

Location: _____

Weather: ☀ ☁ 🌤 🌧 Temperature: _____

The Jump

Type of jump: _____ Aircraft: _____

Equipment: _____

Alt. Exit: _____

Alt. Deployment: _____

Freefall Duration: _____

Total Freefall Time: _____

Signature

☐

Comments & Rating

_____

_____

Overall Rating

⭐ ⭐ ⭐ ⭐ ⭐

SKYDIVE LOG N°

Date: _____ Time: _____

Location: _____

Weather: ☀ ☁ ⛅ 🌧 Temperature: _____

The Jump

Type of jump: _____ Aircraft: _____

Equipment: _____

Alt. Exit: _____

Alt. Deployment: _____

Freefall Duration: _____

Total Freefall Time: _____

Signature

Comments & Rating

_____

_____

_____

Overall Rating

⭐ ⭐ ⭐ ⭐ ⭐

SKYDIVE LOG N°

Date: _____ Time: _____

Location: _____

Weather: ☀ ☁ ⛅ 🌧 Temperature: _____

The Jump

Type of jump: _____ Aircraft: _____

Equipment: _____

Alt. Exit: _____

Alt. Deployment: _____

Freefall Duration: _____

Total Freefall Time: _____

Signature

Comments & Rating

_____

_____

_____

Overall Rating

⭐ ⭐ ⭐ ⭐ ⭐

SKYDIVE LOG

N°

Date: _____ Time: _____

Location: _____

Weather: ☀ ☁ ⛅ 🌧 Temperature: _____

The Jump

Type of jump: _____ Aircraft: _____

Equipment: _____

Alt. Exit: _____

Alt. Deployment: _____

Freefall Duration: _____

Total Freefall Time: _____

Signature

Comments & Rating

_____

_____

_____

Overall Rating

⭐ ⭐ ⭐ ⭐ ⭐

SKYDIVE LOG

N°

Date: _____ Time: _____

Location: _____

Weather: ☀ ☁ ⛅ 🌧 Temperature: _____

The Jump

Type of jump: _____ Aircraft: _____

Equipment: _____

Alt. Exit: _____

Alt. Deployment: _____

Freefall Duration: _____

Total Freefall Time: _____

Signature

Comments & Rating

_____

_____

_____

Overall Rating

⭐ ⭐ ⭐ ⭐ ⭐

SKYDIVE LOG

N° ☐

Date: _____ Time: _____
Location: _____
Weather: ☀ ☁ ⛅ 🌧 Temperature: _____

The Jump

Type of jump: _____ Aircraft: _____
Equipment: _____
Alt. Exit: _____

Signature

Alt. Deployment: _____
Freefall Duration: _____
Total Freefall Time: _____

Comments & Rating

_____
_____   Overall Rating
_____   ★ ★ ★ ★ ★

SKYDIVE LOG

N° ☐

Date: _____ Time: _____
Location: _____
Weather: ☀ ☁ ⛅ 🌧 Temperature: _____

The Jump

Type of jump: _____ Aircraft: _____
Equipment: _____
Alt. Exit: _____

Signature

Alt. Deployment: _____
Freefall Duration: _____
Total Freefall Time: _____

Comments & Rating

_____
_____   Overall Rating
_____   ★ ★ ★ ★ ★

SKYDIVE LOG

N°

Date: _____ Time: _____

Location: _____

Weather: ☀ ☁ 🌤 🌧 Temperature: _____

The Jump

Type of jump: _____ Aircraft: _____

Equipment: _____

Alt. Exit: _____

Alt. Deployment: _____

Freefall Duration: _____

Total Freefall Time: _____

Signature

Comments & Rating

_____
_____

Overall Rating

⭐ ⭐ ⭐ ⭐ ⭐

SKYDIVE LOG

N°

Date: _____ Time: _____

Location: _____

Weather: ☀ ☁ 🌤 🌧 Temperature: _____

The Jump

Type of jump: _____ Aircraft: _____

Equipment: _____

Alt. Exit: _____

Alt. Deployment: _____

Freefall Duration: _____

Total Freefall Time: _____

Signature

Comments & Rating

_____
_____

Overall Rating

⭐ ⭐ ⭐ ⭐ ⭐

Date: _____   Time: _____

Location: _____

Weather: ☀ ☁ ⛅ 🌧 Temperature: _____

The Jump

Type of jump: _____   Aircraft: _____

Equipment: _____

Alt. Exit: _____

Alt. Deployment: _____

Freefall Duration: _____

Total Freefall Time: _____

Signature

Comments & Rating

_____
_____
_____

Overall Rating
⭐ ⭐ ⭐ ⭐ ⭐

SKYDIVE LOG   N°

Date: _____   Time: _____

Location: _____

Weather: ☀ ☁ ⛅ 🌧 Temperature: _____

The Jump

Type of jump: _____   Aircraft: _____

Equipment: _____

Alt. Exit: _____

Alt. Deployment: _____

Freefall Duration: _____

Total Freefall Time: _____

Signature

Comments & Rating

_____
_____
_____

Overall Rating
⭐ ⭐ ⭐ ⭐ ⭐

SKYDIVE LOG

N°

Date: _____ Time: _____

Location: _____

Weather: ☀ ☁ 🌤 🌧 Temperature: _____

The Jump

Type of jump: _____ Aircraft: _____

Equipment: _____

Alt. Exit: _____

Alt. Deployment: _____

Freefall Duration: _____

Total Freefall Time: _____

Signature

Comments & Rating

_____

_____

Overall Rating

⭐ ⭐ ⭐ ⭐ ⭐

SKYDIVE LOG

N°

Date: _____ Time: _____

Location: _____

Weather: ☀ ☁ 🌤 🌧 Temperature: _____

The Jump

Type of jump: _____ Aircraft: _____

Equipment: _____

Alt. Exit: _____

Alt. Deployment: _____

Freefall Duration: _____

Total Freefall Time: _____

Signature

Comments & Rating

_____

_____

Overall Rating

⭐ ⭐ ⭐ ⭐ ⭐

SKYDIVE LOG   N° ☐

Date: _____ Time: _____

Location: _____

Weather: ☀ ☁ 🌤 🌧 Temperature: _____

The Jump

Type of jump: _____ Aircraft: _____

Equipment: _____

Alt. Exit: _____

Alt. Deployment: _____

Freefall Duration: _____

Total Freefall Time: _____

Signature

☐

Comments & Rating

_____

_____

Overall Rating

⭐ ⭐ ⭐ ⭐ ⭐

SKYDIVE LOG   N° ☐

Date: _____ Time: _____

Location: _____

Weather: ☀ ☁ 🌤 🌧 Temperature: _____

The Jump

Type of jump: _____ Aircraft: _____

Equipment: _____

Alt. Exit: _____

Alt. Deployment: _____

Freefall Duration: _____

Total Freefall Time: _____

Signature

☐

Comments & Rating

_____

_____

Overall Rating

⭐ ⭐ ⭐ ⭐ ⭐

SKYDIVE LOG

N°

Date: _____ Time: _____

Location: _____

Weather: ☀ ☁ 🌥 🌧 Temperature: _____

The Jump

Type of jump: _____ Aircraft: _____

Equipment: _____

Alt. Exit: _____

Alt. Deployment: _____

Freefall Duration: _____

Total Freefall Time: _____

Signature

Comments & Rating

_____
_____
_____

Overall Rating
⭐ ⭐ ⭐ ⭐ ⭐

SKYDIVE LOG

N°

Date: _____ Time: _____

Location: _____

Weather: ☀ ☁ 🌥 🌧 Temperature: _____

The Jump

Type of jump: _____ Aircraft: _____

Equipment: _____

Alt. Exit: _____

Alt. Deployment: _____

Freefall Duration: _____

Total Freefall Time: _____

Signature

Comments & Rating

_____
_____
_____

Overall Rating
⭐ ⭐ ⭐ ⭐ ⭐

SKYDIVE LOG N°

Date: _____ Time: _____

Location: _____

Weather: ☀ ☁ ⛅ 🌧 Temperature: _____

The Jump

Type of jump: _____ Aircraft: _____

Equipment: _____

Alt. Exit: _____ Signature

Alt. Deployment: _____

Freefall Duration: _____

Total Freefall Time: _____

Comments & Rating

_____

_____ Overall Rating

_____ ⭐ ⭐ ⭐ ⭐ ⭐

SKYDIVE LOG N°

Date: _____ Time: _____

Location: _____

Weather: ☀ ☁ ⛅ 🌧 Temperature: _____

The Jump

Type of jump: _____ Aircraft: _____

Equipment: _____

Alt. Exit: _____ Signature

Alt. Deployment: _____

Freefall Duration: _____

Total Freefall Time: _____

Comments & Rating

_____

_____ Overall Rating

_____ ⭐ ⭐ ⭐ ⭐ ⭐

SKYDIVE LOG

N°

Date: _____   Time: _____
Location: _____
Weather: ☀ ☁ ⛅ 🌧 Temperature: _____

The Jump

Type of jump: _____ Aircraft: _____
Equipment: _____
Alt. Exit: _____   Signature
Alt. Deployment: _____
Freefall Duration: _____
Total Freefall Time: _____

Comments & Rating

_____
_____   Overall Rating
_____   ★ ★ ★ ★ ★

SKYDIVE LOG

N°

Date: _____   Time: _____
Location: _____
Weather: ☀ ☁ ⛅ 🌧 Temperature: _____

The Jump

Type of jump: _____ Aircraft: _____
Equipment: _____
Alt. Exit: _____   Signature
Alt. Deployment: _____
Freefall Duration: _____
Total Freefall Time: _____

Comments & Rating

_____
_____   Overall Rating
_____   ★ ★ ★ ★ ★

SKYDIVE LOG   N° ☐

Date: _____   Time: _____

Location: _____

Weather: ☀ ☁ ⛅ 🌧 Temperature: _____

The Jump

Type of jump: _____ Aircraft: _____

Equipment: _____

Alt. Exit: _____   Signature

Alt. Deployment: _____

Freefall Duration: _____

Total Freefall Time: _____

Comments & Rating

_____   Overall Rating

_____   ⭐ ⭐ ⭐ ⭐ ⭐

_____

SKYDIVE LOG   N° ☐

Date: _____   Time: _____

Location: _____

Weather: ☀ ☁ ⛅ 🌧 Temperature: _____

The Jump

Type of jump: _____ Aircraft: _____

Equipment: _____

Alt. Exit: _____   Signature

Alt. Deployment: _____

Freefall Duration: _____

Total Freefall Time: _____

Comments & Rating

_____   Overall Rating

_____   ⭐ ⭐ ⭐ ⭐ ⭐

_____

SKYDIVE LOG

N° ☐

Date: _____ Time: _____
Location: _____
Weather: ☀ ☁ ⛅ 🌧 Temperature: _____

The Jump

Type of jump: _____ Aircraft: _____
Equipment: _____
Alt. Exit: _____ Signature
Alt. Deployment: _____
Freefall Duration: _____ ☐
Total Freefall Time: _____

Comments & Rating

_____ Overall Rating
_____ ⭐ ⭐ ⭐ ⭐ ⭐
_____

SKYDIVE LOG

N° ☐

Date: _____ Time: _____
Location: _____
Weather: ☀ ☁ ⛅ 🌧 Temperature: _____

The Jump

Type of jump: _____ Aircraft: _____
Equipment: _____
Alt. Exit: _____ Signature
Alt. Deployment: _____
Freefall Duration: _____ ☐
Total Freefall Time: _____

Comments & Rating

_____ Overall Rating
_____ ⭐ ⭐ ⭐ ⭐ ⭐
_____

SKYDIVE LOG N°

Date: _____ Time: _____
Location: _____
Weather: ☀ ☁ ⛅ 🌧 Temperature: _____

The Jump

Type of jump: _____ Aircraft: _____
Equipment: _____
Alt. Exit: _____
Alt. Deployment: _____ Signature
Freefall Duration: _____
Total Freefall Time: _____

Comments & Rating

_____
_____ Overall Rating
_____ ★ ★ ★ ★ ★

SKYDIVE LOG N°

Date: _____ Time: _____
Location: _____
Weather: ☀ ☁ ⛅ 🌧 Temperature: _____

The Jump

Type of jump: _____ Aircraft: _____
Equipment: _____
Alt. Exit: _____
Alt. Deployment: _____ Signature
Freefall Duration: _____
Total Freefall Time: _____

Comments & Rating

_____
_____ Overall Rating
_____ ★ ★ ★ ★ ★

SKYDIVE LOG

N°

Date: _____ Time: _____

Location: _____

Weather: ☀ ☁ ⛅ 🌧 Temperature: _____

The Jump

Type of jump: _____ Aircraft: _____

Equipment: _____

Alt. Exit: _____

Alt. Deployment: _____

Freefall Duration: _____

Total Freefall Time: _____

Signature

Comments & Rating

_____

_____

_____

Overall Rating

⭐ ⭐ ⭐ ⭐ ⭐

SKYDIVE LOG

N°

Date: _____ Time: _____

Location: _____

Weather: ☀ ☁ ⛅ 🌧 Temperature: _____

The Jump

Type of jump: _____ Aircraft: _____

Equipment: _____

Alt. Exit: _____

Alt. Deployment: _____

Freefall Duration: _____

Total Freefall Time: _____

Signature

Comments & Rating

_____

_____

_____

Overall Rating

⭐ ⭐ ⭐ ⭐ ⭐

SKYDIVE LOG

N°

Date: _____ Time: _____

Location: _____

Weather: ☀ ☁ ⛅ 🌧 Temperature: _____

The Jump

Type of jump: _____ Aircraft: _____

Equipment: _____

Alt. Exit: _____

Alt. Deployment: _____

Freefall Duration: _____

Total Freefall Time: _____

Signature

Comments & Rating

_____

_____

_____

Overall Rating

⭐ ⭐ ⭐ ⭐ ⭐

SKYDIVE LOG

N°

Date: _____ Time: _____

Location: _____

Weather: ☀ ☁ ⛅ 🌧 Temperature: _____

The Jump

Type of jump: _____ Aircraft: _____

Equipment: _____

Alt. Exit: _____

Alt. Deployment: _____

Freefall Duration: _____

Total Freefall Time: _____

Signature

Comments & Rating

_____

_____

_____

Overall Rating

⭐ ⭐ ⭐ ⭐ ⭐

SKYDIVE LOG   N°

Date: _____ Time: _____

Location: _____

Weather: ☀ ☁ ⛅ 🌧 Temperature: _____

The Jump

Type of jump: _____ Aircraft: _____

Equipment: _____

Alt. Exit: _____   Signature

Alt. Deployment: _____

Freefall Duration: _____

Total Freefall Time: _____

Comments & Rating

_____   Overall Rating

_____   ⭐ ⭐ ⭐ ⭐ ⭐

_____

SKYDIVE LOG   N°

Date: _____ Time: _____

Location: _____

Weather: ☀ ☁ ⛅ 🌧 Temperature: _____

The Jump

Type of jump: _____ Aircraft: _____

Equipment: _____

Alt. Exit: _____   Signature

Alt. Deployment: _____

Freefall Duration: _____

Total Freefall Time: _____

Comments & Rating

_____   Overall Rating

_____   ⭐ ⭐ ⭐ ⭐ ⭐

_____

SKYDIVE LOG N°

Date: _____ Time: _____

Location: _____

Weather: ☀ ☁ ⛅ 🌧 Temperature: _____

The Jump

Type of jump: _____ Aircraft: _____

Equipment: _____

Alt. Exit: _____ Signature

Alt. Deployment: _____

Freefall Duration: _____

Total Freefall Time: _____

Comments & Rating

_____

_____ Overall Rating

_____ ⭐⭐⭐⭐⭐

SKYDIVE LOG N°

Date: _____ Time: _____

Location: _____

Weather: ☀ ☁ ⛅ 🌧 Temperature: _____

The Jump

Type of jump: _____ Aircraft: _____

Equipment: _____

Alt. Exit: _____ Signature

Alt. Deployment: _____

Freefall Duration: _____

Total Freefall Time: _____

Comments & Rating

_____

_____ Overall Rating

_____ ⭐⭐⭐⭐⭐

SKYDIVE LOG N°

Date: _____ Time: _____

Location: _____

Weather: ☀ ☁ 🌥 🌧 Temperature: _____

The Jump

Type of jump: _____ Aircraft: _____

Equipment: _____

Alt. Exit: _____ Signature

Alt. Deployment: _____

Freefall Duration: _____

Total Freefall Time: _____

Comments & Rating

_____ Overall Rating

_____ ⭐ ⭐ ⭐ ⭐ ⭐

_____

SKYDIVE LOG N°

Date: _____ Time: _____

Location: _____

Weather: ☀ ☁ 🌥 🌧 Temperature: _____

The Jump

Type of jump: _____ Aircraft: _____

Equipment: _____

Alt. Exit: _____ Signature

Alt. Deployment: _____

Freefall Duration: _____

Total Freefall Time: _____

Comments & Rating

_____ Overall Rating

_____ ⭐ ⭐ ⭐ ⭐ ⭐

_____

SKYDIVE LOG
N° ☐

Date: _____ Time: _____

Location: _____

Weather: ☀ ☁ ⛅ 🌧 Temperature: _____

The Jump

Type of jump: _____ Aircraft: _____

Equipment: _____

Alt. Exit: _____

Alt. Deployment: _____

Freefall Duration: _____

Total Freefall Time: _____

Signature

☐

Comments & Rating

_____

_____

_____

Overall Rating

☆ ☆ ☆ ☆ ☆

SKYDIVE LOG
N° ☐

Date: _____ Time: _____

Location: _____

Weather: ☀ ☁ ⛅ 🌧 Temperature: _____

The Jump

Type of jump: _____ Aircraft: _____

Equipment: _____

Alt. Exit: _____

Alt. Deployment: _____

Freefall Duration: _____

Total Freefall Time: _____

Signature

☐

Comments & Rating

_____

_____

_____

Overall Rating

☆ ☆ ☆ ☆ ☆

SKYDIVE LOG N°

Date: _____ Time: _____

Location: _____

Weather: ☀ ☁ ⛅ 🌧 Temperature: _____

The Jump

Type of jump: _____ Aircraft: _____

Equipment: _____

Alt. Exit: _____

Alt. Deployment: _____

Freefall Duration: _____

Total Freefall Time: _____

Signature

Comments & Rating

_____

_____

_____

Overall Rating

⭐ ⭐ ⭐ ⭐ ⭐

SKYDIVE LOG N°

Date: _____ Time: _____

Location: _____

Weather: ☀ ☁ ⛅ 🌧 Temperature: _____

The Jump

Type of jump: _____ Aircraft: _____

Equipment: _____

Alt. Exit: _____

Alt. Deployment: _____

Freefall Duration: _____

Total Freefall Time: _____

Signature

Comments & Rating

_____

_____

_____

Overall Rating

⭐ ⭐ ⭐ ⭐ ⭐

Date: _____ Time: _____

Location: _____

Weather: ☀ ☁ ⛅ 🌧 Temperature: _____

The Jump

Type of jump: _____ Aircraft: _____

Equipment: _____

Alt. Exit: _____

Alt. Deployment: _____

Freefall Duration: _____

Total Freefall Time: _____

Signature

Comments & Rating

_____

_____

_____

Overall Rating

⭐ ⭐ ⭐ ⭐ ⭐

SKYDIVE LOG N°

Date: _____ Time: _____

Location: _____

Weather: ☀ ☁ ⛅ 🌧 Temperature: _____

The Jump

Type of jump: _____ Aircraft: _____

Equipment: _____

Alt. Exit: _____

Alt. Deployment: _____

Freefall Duration: _____

Total Freefall Time: _____

Signature

Comments & Rating

_____

_____

_____

Overall Rating

⭐ ⭐ ⭐ ⭐ ⭐

SKYDIVE LOG

N°

Date: _____ Time: _____

Location: _____

Weather: ☀ ☁ 🌤 🌧 Temperature: _____

The Jump

Type of jump: _____ Aircraft: _____

Equipment: _____

Alt. Exit: _____

Alt. Deployment: _____

Freefall Duration: _____

Total Freefall Time: _____

Signature

Comments & Rating

_____

_____

_____

Overall Rating

★ ★ ★ ★ ★

SKYDIVE LOG

N°

Date: _____ Time: _____

Location: _____

Weather: ☀ ☁ 🌤 🌧 Temperature: _____

The Jump

Type of jump: _____ Aircraft: _____

Equipment: _____

Alt. Exit: _____

Alt. Deployment: _____

Freefall Duration: _____

Total Freefall Time: _____

Signature

Comments & Rating

_____

_____

_____

Overall Rating

★ ★ ★ ★ ★

SKYDIVE LOG   N° ☐

Date: _____ Time: _____

Location: _____

Weather: ☀ ☁ ⛅ 🌧 Temperature: _____

The Jump

Type of jump: _____ Aircraft: _____

Equipment: _____

Alt. Exit: _____

Alt. Deployment: _____   Signature

Freefall Duration: _____   ┌─────────┐
                                             │   │
Total Freefall Time: _____   │   │
                                             └─────────┘

Comments & Rating

_____   Overall Rating

_____   ☆ ☆ ☆ ☆ ☆

_____

SKYDIVE LOG   N° ☐

Date: _____ Time: _____

Location: _____

Weather: ☀ ☁ ⛅ 🌧 Temperature: _____

The Jump

Type of jump: _____ Aircraft: _____

Equipment: _____

Alt. Exit: _____

Alt. Deployment: _____   Signature

Freefall Duration: _____   ┌─────────┐
                                             │   │
Total Freefall Time: _____   │   │
                                             └─────────┘

Comments & Rating

_____   Overall Rating

_____   ☆ ☆ ☆ ☆ ☆

_____

SKYDIVE LOG   N° ☐

Date: _____ Time: _____

Location: _____

Weather: ☀ ☁ ⛅ 🌧 Temperature: _____

The Jump

Type of jump: _____ Aircraft: _____

Equipment: _____

Alt. Exit: _____

Alt. Deployment: _____   Signature

Freefall Duration: _____

Total Freefall Time: _____

Comments & Rating

_____   Overall Rating

_____   ★ ★ ★ ★ ★

_____

SKYDIVE LOG   N° ☐

Date: _____ Time: _____

Location: _____

Weather: ☀ ☁ ⛅ 🌧 Temperature: _____

The Jump

Type of jump: _____ Aircraft: _____

Equipment: _____

Alt. Exit: _____

Alt. Deployment: _____   Signature

Freefall Duration: _____

Total Freefall Time: _____

Comments & Rating

_____   Overall Rating

_____   ★ ★ ★ ★ ★

_____

SKYDIVE LOG N° ☐

Date: _____ Time: _____

Location: _____

Weather: ☀ ☁ ⛅ 🌧 Temperature: _____

The Jump

Type of jump: _____ Aircraft: _____

Equipment: _____

Alt. Exit: _____

Alt. Deployment: _____ Signature

Freefall Duration: _____

Total Freefall Time: _____

Comments & Rating

_____

_____   Overall Rating

_____   ⭐ ⭐ ⭐ ⭐ ⭐

SKYDIVE LOG N° ☐

Date: _____ Time: _____

Location: _____

Weather: ☀ ☁ ⛅ 🌧 Temperature: _____

The Jump

Type of jump: _____ Aircraft: _____

Equipment: _____

Alt. Exit: _____

Alt. Deployment: _____ Signature

Freefall Duration: _____

Total Freefall Time: _____

Comments & Rating

_____

_____   Overall Rating

_____   ⭐ ⭐ ⭐ ⭐ ⭐

SKYDIVE LOG N°

Date: _____ Time: _____

Location: _____

Weather: ☀ ☁ ⛅ 🌧 Temperature: _____

The Jump

Type of jump: _____ Aircraft: _____

Equipment: _____

Alt. Exit: _____

Alt. Deployment: _____

Freefall Duration: _____

Total Freefall Time: _____

Signature

Comments & Rating

_____

_____

_____

Overall Rating

⭐ ⭐ ⭐ ⭐ ⭐

SKYDIVE LOG N°

Date: _____ Time: _____

Location: _____

Weather: ☀ ☁ ⛅ 🌧 Temperature: _____

The Jump

Type of jump: _____ Aircraft: _____

Equipment: _____

Alt. Exit: _____

Alt. Deployment: _____

Freefall Duration: _____

Total Freefall Time: _____

Signature

Comments & Rating

_____

_____

_____

Overall Rating

⭐ ⭐ ⭐ ⭐ ⭐

SKYDIVE LOG   N° ☐

Date: _____   Time: _____

Location: _____

Weather: ☀ ☁ ⛅ 🌧 Temperature: _____

The Jump

Type of jump: _____ Aircraft: _____

Equipment: _____

Alt. Exit: _____   Signature

Alt. Deployment: _____

Freefall Duration: _____

Total Freefall Time: _____

Comments & Rating

_____   Overall Rating

_____   ⭐ ⭐ ⭐ ⭐ ⭐

_____

SKYDIVE LOG   N° ☐

Date: _____   Time: _____

Location: _____

Weather: ☀ ☁ ⛅ 🌧 Temperature: _____

The Jump

Type of jump: _____ Aircraft: _____

Equipment: _____

Alt. Exit: _____   Signature

Alt. Deployment: _____

Freefall Duration: _____

Total Freefall Time: _____

Comments & Rating

_____   Overall Rating

_____   ⭐ ⭐ ⭐ ⭐ ⭐

_____

SKYDIVE LOG

N° ☐

Date: _____ Time: _____

Location: _____

Weather: ☀ ☁ ⛅ 🌧 Temperature: _____

The Jump

Type of jump: _____ Aircraft: _____

Equipment: _____

Alt. Exit: _____

Alt. Deployment: _____

Freefall Duration: _____

Total Freefall Time: _____

Signature

☐

Comments & Rating

_____
_____
_____

Overall Rating

⭐ ⭐ ⭐ ⭐ ⭐

SKYDIVE LOG

N° ☐

Date: _____ Time: _____

Location: _____

Weather: ☀ ☁ ⛅ 🌧 Temperature: _____

The Jump

Type of jump: _____ Aircraft: _____

Equipment: _____

Alt. Exit: _____

Alt. Deployment: _____

Freefall Duration: _____

Total Freefall Time: _____

Signature

☐

Comments & Rating

_____
_____
_____

Overall Rating

⭐ ⭐ ⭐ ⭐ ⭐

SKYDIVE LOG N° ☐

Date: _____ Time: _____

Location: _____

Weather: ☀ ☁ ⛅ 🌧 Temperature: _____

The Jump

Type of jump: _____ Aircraft: _____

Equipment: _____

Alt. Exit: _____

Alt. Deployment: _____

Freefall Duration: _____

Total Freefall Time: _____

Signature

☐

Comments & Rating

_____

_____

_____

Overall Rating

⭐ ⭐ ⭐ ⭐ ⭐

SKYDIVE LOG N° ☐

Date: _____ Time: _____

Location: _____

Weather: ☀ ☁ ⛅ 🌧 Temperature: _____

The Jump

Type of jump: _____ Aircraft: _____

Equipment: _____

Alt. Exit: _____

Alt. Deployment: _____

Freefall Duration: _____

Total Freefall Time: _____

Signature

☐

Comments & Rating

_____

_____

_____

Overall Rating

⭐ ⭐ ⭐ ⭐ ⭐

SKYDIVE LOG

N°

Date: _____ Time: _____
Location: _____
Weather: ☀ ☁ ⛅ 🌧 Temperature: _____

The Jump

Type of jump: _____ Aircraft: _____
Equipment: _____
Alt. Exit: _____

Signature

Alt. Deployment: _____
Freefall Duration: _____
Total Freefall Time: _____

Comments & Rating

_____
_____   Overall Rating
_____   ⭐ ⭐ ⭐ ⭐ ⭐

SKYDIVE LOG

N°

Date: _____ Time: _____
Location: _____
Weather: ☀ ☁ ⛅ 🌧 Temperature: _____

The Jump

Type of jump: _____ Aircraft: _____
Equipment: _____
Alt. Exit: _____

Signature

Alt. Deployment: _____
Freefall Duration: _____
Total Freefall Time: _____

Comments & Rating

_____
_____   Overall Rating
_____   ⭐ ⭐ ⭐ ⭐ ⭐

SKYDIVE LOG   N°

Date: _____ Time: _____

Location: _____

Weather: ☀ ☁ ⛅ 🌧 Temperature: _____

The Jump

Type of jump: _____ Aircraft: _____

Equipment: _____

Alt. Exit: _____   Signature

Alt. Deployment: _____

Freefall Duration: _____

Total Freefall Time: _____

Comments & Rating

_____
_____   Overall Rating
_____   ⭐ ⭐ ⭐ ⭐ ⭐

SKYDIVE LOG   N°

Date: _____ Time: _____

Location: _____

Weather: ☀ ☁ ⛅ 🌧 Temperature: _____

The Jump

Type of jump: _____ Aircraft: _____

Equipment: _____

Alt. Exit: _____   Signature

Alt. Deployment: _____

Freefall Duration: _____

Total Freefall Time: _____

Comments & Rating

_____
_____   Overall Rating
_____   ⭐ ⭐ ⭐ ⭐ ⭐

SKYDIVE LOG   N° ☐

Date: _____ Time: _____

Location: _____

Weather: ☀ ☁ ⛅ 🌧 Temperature: _____

The Jump

Type of jump: _____ Aircraft: _____

Equipment: _____

Alt. Exit: _____   Signature

Alt. Deployment: _____

Freefall Duration: _____

Total Freefall Time: _____

Comments & Rating

_____   Overall Rating

_____   ⭐ ⭐ ⭐ ⭐ ⭐

_____

SKYDIVE LOG   N° ☐

Date: _____ Time: _____

Location: _____

Weather: ☀ ☁ ⛅ 🌧 Temperature: _____

The Jump

Type of jump: _____ Aircraft: _____

Equipment: _____

Alt. Exit: _____   Signature

Alt. Deployment: _____

Freefall Duration: _____

Total Freefall Time: _____

Comments & Rating

_____   Overall Rating

_____   ⭐ ⭐ ⭐ ⭐ ⭐

_____

SKYDIVE LOG   N° ☐

Date: _____   Time: _____
Location: _____
Weather: ☀ ☁ ⛅ 🌧 Temperature: _____

The Jump

Type of jump: _____ Aircraft: _____
Equipment: _____
Alt. Exit: _____
Alt. Deployment: _____   Signature
Freefall Duration: _____
Total Freefall Time: _____

Comments & Rating

_____   Overall Rating
_____   ★ ★ ★ ★ ★
_____

SKYDIVE LOG   N° ☐

Date: _____   Time: _____
Location: _____
Weather: ☀ ☁ ⛅ 🌧 Temperature: _____

The Jump

Type of jump: _____ Aircraft: _____
Equipment: _____
Alt. Exit: _____
Alt. Deployment: _____   Signature
Freefall Duration: _____
Total Freefall Time: _____

Comments & Rating

_____   Overall Rating
_____   ★ ★ ★ ★ ★
_____

SKYDIVE LOG N°

Date: _____ Time: _____
Location: _____
Weather: ☀ ☁ 🌤 🌧 Temperature: _____

The Jump

Type of jump: _____ Aircraft: _____
Equipment: _____
Alt. Exit: _____
Alt. Deployment: _____
Freefall Duration: _____
Total Freefall Time: _____

Signature

Comments & Rating

_____
_____
_____

Overall Rating
⭐ ⭐ ⭐ ⭐ ⭐

SKYDIVE LOG N°

Date: _____ Time: _____
Location: _____
Weather: ☀ ☁ 🌤 🌧 Temperature: _____

The Jump

Type of jump: _____ Aircraft: _____
Equipment: _____
Alt. Exit: _____
Alt. Deployment: _____
Freefall Duration: _____
Total Freefall Time: _____

Signature

Comments & Rating

_____
_____
_____

Overall Rating
⭐ ⭐ ⭐ ⭐ ⭐

SKYDIVE LOG N° ▢

Date: _____ Time: _____

Location: _____

Weather: ☀ ☁ ⛅ 🌧 Temperature: _____

The Jump

Type of jump: _____ Aircraft: _____

Equipment: _____

Alt. Exit: _____ **Signature**

Alt. Deployment: _____

Freefall Duration: _____

Total Freefall Time: _____

Comments & Rating

_____ **Overall Rating**
_____
_____ ★ ★ ★ ★ ★

SKYDIVE LOG N° ▢

Date: _____ Time: _____

Location: _____

Weather: ☀ ☁ ⛅ 🌧 Temperature: _____

The Jump

Type of jump: _____ Aircraft: _____

Equipment: _____

Alt. Exit: _____ **Signature**

Alt. Deployment: _____

Freefall Duration: _____

Total Freefall Time: _____

Comments & Rating

_____ **Overall Rating**
_____
_____ ★ ★ ★ ★ ★

SKYDIVE LOG N°

Date: _____ Time: _____

Location: _____

Weather: ☀ ☁ ⛅ 🌧 Temperature: _____

The Jump

Type of jump: _____ Aircraft: _____

Equipment: _____

Alt. Exit: _____

Alt. Deployment: _____

Freefall Duration: _____

Total Freefall Time: _____

Signature

Comments & Rating

_____

_____

_____

Overall Rating

★ ★ ★ ★ ★

SKYDIVE LOG N°

Date: _____ Time: _____

Location: _____

Weather: ☀ ☁ ⛅ 🌧 Temperature: _____

The Jump

Type of jump: _____ Aircraft: _____

Equipment: _____

Alt. Exit: _____

Alt. Deployment: _____

Freefall Duration: _____

Total Freefall Time: _____

Signature

Comments & Rating

_____

_____

_____

Overall Rating

★ ★ ★ ★ ★

SKYDIVE LOG   N° ☐

Date: _____ Time: _____

Location: _____

Weather: ☀ ☁ ⛅ 🌧 Temperature: _____

The Jump

Type of jump: _____ Aircraft: _____

Equipment: _____

Alt. Exit: _____

Alt. Deployment: _____   Signature

Freefall Duration: _____

Total Freefall Time: _____

Comments & Rating

_____   Overall Rating

_____   ★ ★ ★ ★ ★

_____

SKYDIVE LOG   N° ☐

Date: _____ Time: _____

Location: _____

Weather: ☀ ☁ ⛅ 🌧 Temperature: _____

The Jump

Type of jump: _____ Aircraft: _____

Equipment: _____

Alt. Exit: _____

Alt. Deployment: _____   Signature

Freefall Duration: _____

Total Freefall Time: _____

Comments & Rating

_____   Overall Rating

_____   ★ ★ ★ ★ ★

_____

SKYDIVE LOG

N°

Date: _____ Time: _____

Location: _____

Weather: ☀ ☁ ⛅ 🌧 Temperature: _____

The Jump

Type of jump: _____ Aircraft: _____

Equipment: _____

Alt. Exit: _____

Alt. Deployment: _____

Freefall Duration: _____

Total Freefall Time: _____

Signature

Comments & Rating

_____

_____

_____

Overall Rating

⭐ ⭐ ⭐ ⭐ ⭐

SKYDIVE LOG

N°

Date: _____ Time: _____

Location: _____

Weather: ☀ ☁ ⛅ 🌧 Temperature: _____

The Jump

Type of jump: _____ Aircraft: _____

Equipment: _____

Alt. Exit: _____

Alt. Deployment: _____

Freefall Duration: _____

Total Freefall Time: _____

Signature

Comments & Rating

_____

_____

_____

Overall Rating

⭐ ⭐ ⭐ ⭐ ⭐

SKYDIVE LOG N°

Date: _____ Time: _____

Location: _____

Weather: ☀ ☁ ⛅ 🌧 Temperature: _____

The Jump

Type of jump: _____ Aircraft: _____

Equipment: _____

Alt. Exit: _____ Signature

Alt. Deployment: _____

Freefall Duration: _____

Total Freefall Time: _____

Comments & Rating

_____ Overall Rating

_____ ⭐ ⭐ ⭐ ⭐ ⭐

_____

SKYDIVE LOG N°

Date: _____ Time: _____

Location: _____

Weather: ☀ ☁ ⛅ 🌧 Temperature: _____

The Jump

Type of jump: _____ Aircraft: _____

Equipment: _____

Alt. Exit: _____ Signature

Alt. Deployment: _____

Freefall Duration: _____

Total Freefall Time: _____

Comments & Rating

_____ Overall Rating

_____ ⭐ ⭐ ⭐ ⭐ ⭐

_____

SKYDIVE LOG

N°

Date: _____ Time: _____

Location: _____

Weather: ☀ ☁ ⛅ 🌧 Temperature: _____

The Jump

Type of jump: _____ Aircraft: _____

Equipment: _____

Alt. Exit: _____

Alt. Deployment: _____

Freefall Duration: _____

Total Freefall Time: _____

Signature

Comments & Rating

_____

_____

_____

Overall Rating

⭐ ⭐ ⭐ ⭐ ⭐

SKYDIVE LOG

N°

Date: _____ Time: _____

Location: _____

Weather: ☀ ☁ ⛅ 🌧 Temperature: _____

The Jump

Type of jump: _____ Aircraft: _____

Equipment: _____

Alt. Exit: _____

Alt. Deployment: _____

Freefall Duration: _____

Total Freefall Time: _____

Signature

Comments & Rating

_____

_____

_____

Overall Rating

⭐ ⭐ ⭐ ⭐ ⭐

SKYDIVE LOG   N° ☐

Date: _____ Time: _____

Location: _____

Weather: ☀ ☁ ⛅ 🌧 Temperature: _____

The Jump

Type of jump: _____ Aircraft: _____

Equipment: _____

Alt. Exit: _____

Alt. Deployment: _____

Freefall Duration: _____

Total Freefall Time: _____

Signature

Comments & Rating

_____

_____

_____

Overall Rating

⭐ ⭐ ⭐ ⭐ ⭐

SKYDIVE LOG   N° ☐

Date: _____ Time: _____

Location: _____

Weather: ☀ ☁ ⛅ 🌧 Temperature: _____

The Jump

Type of jump: _____ Aircraft: _____

Equipment: _____

Alt. Exit: _____

Alt. Deployment: _____

Freefall Duration: _____

Total Freefall Time: _____

Signature

Comments & Rating

_____

_____

_____

Overall Rating

⭐ ⭐ ⭐ ⭐ ⭐

45171814R00051